# The Splendor of Window Boxes

An Emma Rose Sparrow Book

Copyright © 2015 Emma Rose Sparrow
All rights reserved.
Publish Date: November 12, 2015

Editor-in-Chief: Connor Chagnon
Sterling Elle Publishing
Bradford, Massachusetts

ISBN-13:978-1519302892
ISBN-10:1519302894

# Photo Credits

The artist/source credits for the photos in this book are listed in the order in which they appear:

Cover: Robert Crum/Shutterstock
Gail Johnson/Shutterstock
Helmut Konrad Watson/Shutterstock
Shutterschock/Shutterstock
PHB.cz (Richard Semik)/Shutterstock
Susan Drew/Shutterstock
Malgorzata Kistryn/Shutterstock
David Kay/Shutterstock
Ann W. Kosche/Shutterstock
Anne Kitzman/Shutterstock
Greg Wolford/Shutterstock
Thampapon/Shutterstock
Alexandra Giese/Shutterstock
Poly Liss/Shutterstock
davidelliottphotos/Shutterstock
wjarek/Shutterstock
romakoma/Shutterstock
kengphotostock/Shutterstock
Pabl1n/Shutterstock
Sutichak Yachiangkham/Shutterstock
S.H.E./Shutterstock
Milosz_M/Shutterstock
Omegafoto/Shutterstock
Alexander Mazurkevich/Shutterstock
Volker Rauch/Shutterstock
Lovethief/Shutterstock
Gergely Zsolnai/Shutterstock
Lek Changply/Shutterstock
Souchon Yves/Shutterstock
Miran Muhic/Shutterstock
Everything/Shutterstock
Gabriele Maltinti/Shutterstock
Cebas/Shutterstock
InnaFelker/Shutterstock
imagedb.com/Shutterstock
Gabriele Maltinti/Shutterstock
Carlo Villa/Shutterstock
Martina Ebel/Shutterstock
JD Photograph/Shutterstock
Vladislav T. Jirousek/Shutterstock
Alexandra Giese/Shutterstock
Dziewul/Shutterstock
Randall Vermillion/Shutterstock
Sutichak Yachiangkham/Shutterstock
Dora Zett/Shutterstock

Made in the USA
Columbia, SC
26 February 2019